Contents

Chapter 1: Understanding Trauma

Chapter 2: Self-Exploration and Awareness

Chapter 3: Building Resilience

Chapter 4: Processing and Expressing Emotions

Chapter 5: Healing Through Forgiveness

Chapter 6: Moving Forward and Thriving

Chapter 7: Sustaining Your Healing Journey

Chapter 1: Understanding Trauma

What is Trauma?

Trauma is a word that is often thrown around in conversation, but what does it really mean? In the context of healing from past trauma through self-work, it is important to understand the true definition of trauma. Trauma is a deeply distressing or disturbing experience that leaves a lasting impact on an individual's mental, emotional, and physical well-being. It can be caused by a wide range of events, from childhood abuse to natural disasters, and everything in between. Trauma can manifest in many ways, including anxiety, depression, PTSD, and a host of other symptoms. It is crucial to recognize the signs of trauma to begin the healing process.

One of the key aspects of trauma is that it is not always immediately apparent. Trauma can lie dormant within an individual for years, surfacing only when triggered by certain events or memories. This is why self-work is so important in the healing process. By taking the time to explore your past experiences, emotions, and beliefs, you can begin to uncover the root causes of your trauma and start to heal from within. Self-work is a powerful tool for healing, as it allows you to take control of your own healing journey and work through your trauma at your own pace.

Healing from trauma is not a linear process, and it is important to be patient and kind to yourself along the way. Trauma recovery is a journey that requires time, effort, and dedication, but the rewards are well worth it. By engaging in self-work practices such as therapy, journaling, mindfulness, and other healing modalities, you can begin to untangle the web of trauma that has been holding you back and move towards a place of healing and wholeness. Remember that healing is possible, and that you have the strength and resilience within you to overcome your past trauma and create a brighter future for yourself. The willingness to heal first starts in the mind.

Trauma is a complex and deep-rooted experience that can have a lasting impact on our lives. By engaging in self-work practices and taking the time to explore our past experiences, emotions, and beliefs, we can begin to heal from within and move towards a place of healing and wholeness. Remember to be patient and kind to yourself along the way, and to reach out for support when needed. Healing is possible, and you have the power within you to overcome your past trauma and create a brighter future for yourself and for next generations to come.

Types of Traumas

In the journey towards healing from past trauma, it is important to understand the different types of traumas that one may have experienced. By recognizing and acknowledging the specific type of trauma that has impacted our lives, we can begin to address it more effectively and work towards healing and recovery.

One common type of trauma is known as acute trauma, which occurs as a result of a single, highly distressing event such as a car accident that has disrupted your life, natural disaster, traumatic physical abuse or losing a loved one suddenly. Acute trauma can have a significant impact on our mental and emotional well-being, and it is important to seek support and guidance in processing and healing from this type of trauma.

Another type of trauma is known as complex trauma, which is often the result of prolonged exposure to traumatic events such as childhood abuse, neglect, being in toxic relationships or an abusive unhealthy marriage. Complex trauma can have long-lasting effects on our sense of self and our ability to trust others, making it essential to engage in self-work practices that address the deep-rooted wounds caused by this type of trauma.

Additionally, there is intergenerational trauma, which is the transmission of trauma from one generation to another. This type of trauma can manifest in patterns of behaviour, beliefs, and coping mechanisms that have been passed down through families. By recognizing and unpacking intergenerational trauma, we can begin to break the cycle and heal ourselves and future generations to come.

Lastly, there is vicarious trauma, which occurs when we are exposed to the trauma of others, such as through our work as first responders or healthcare professionals. Vicarious trauma can have a profound impact on our mental health and well-being, and it is crucial to engage in selfcare practices that help us process and cope with the secondary trauma we may experience.

By understanding the different types of traumas that can impact our lives, we can begin to take steps towards healing and recovery. Through self-work practices such as therapy, mindfulness, and self-compassion, we can cultivate resilience and strength as we navigate the path to healing from past trauma. Remember, healing is possible, and you are deserving of the peace and healing that you seek.

The Impact of Trauma on the Mind and Body

Trauma has a profound impact on both the mind and body, leaving lasting scars that can hinder our ability to live fully in the present moment. The experiences we have endured shape our perceptions of ourselves and the world around us, creating deep-seated beliefs that can hold us back from reaching our full potential. In order to heal from past trauma, it is essential to understand the ways in which it has affected us.

Our minds are powerful tools that can either help us heal or keep us stuck in a cycle of pain and suffering. Trauma can lead to a wide range of mental health issues, including anxiety, depression, and PTSD. These conditions can make it difficult to navigate everyday life, leading to feelings of isolation and hopelessness. By acknowledging the impact of trauma on our minds, we can begin to take steps towards healing and reclaiming our sense of self-worth. The body also plays a crucial role in trauma recovery, as our physical health is intimately connected to our emotional well-being. Trauma can manifest in physical symptoms such as chronic pain, fatigue, insomnia, digestive issues and various others. These symptoms are often a manifestation of the emotional pain we carry within us and can serve as a powerful reminder of the trauma we have experienced. By tuning into our bodies and listening to their messages, we can begin to release the tension and pain that has been stored within us for so long.

Healing from past trauma through self-work is a journey that requires courage, patience, and self-compassion. It is a process of unravelling the layers of pain and suffering that have accumulated over time, and finding the strength within us to face our deepest wounds. By delving deep into our inner selves and confronting the darkness that lies within, we can begin to heal and transform our lives in profound ways. As we embark on the path to healing, it is important to remember that we are not alone in our journey. There are countless resources and support systems available to help us along the way, from therapy to self-help books and mindfulness practices. By connecting with others who have walked a similar path, we can find solace in knowing that we are not alone in our struggles, and that healing is possible for each one of us.

Chapter 2: Self-Exploration and Awareness

Reflecting on Your Past Experiences

Reflecting on your past experiences is a crucial step on the path to healing from trauma. It allows you to gain a deeper understanding of how your past has shaped your present and provides valuable insights into the patterns and behaviours that may be holding you back. By taking the time to reflect on your past experiences however hard it may be, you can begin to identify the root causes of your trauma and start to work through them in a healthy and productive way.

When reflecting on your past experiences, it's important to approach the process with an open mind and a compassionate heart. Be gentle with yourself as you revisit painful memories and remember that healing is a journey that takes time and patience. Allow yourself to feel whatever emotions come up during this process, whether it's anger, sadness, or fear. By acknowledging and processing these emotions, you can begin to release the hold that the past has on you.

As you reflect on your past experiences, consider seeking out the support of a therapist or counsellor who can help guide you through the healing process. They can provide you with tools and techniques to help you navigate through your past trauma in a healthy and constructive way. Additionally, connecting with others who have experienced similar trauma can provide you with a sense of community and understanding that can be incredibly healing.

Remember that healing from trauma is a deeply personal journey, and there is no one-size-fits all approach. Trust in your own inner wisdom and intuition as you reflect on your past experiences and take steps towards healing. By doing the self-work necessary to heal, you are taking an important step towards reclaiming your power and living a life that is full of joy, peace, and fulfilment.

In conclusion, reflecting on your past experiences is a powerful tool for healing. By approaching this process with an open heart and mind and then trusting in your own inner wisdom, you can begin to release the hold that your past trauma has on you. Remember, healing is a lifelong journey and it is never too late to start the work necessary to reclaim your power and live a life that is free from the shadows of the past.

Identifying Triggers and Patterns

To embark on the path to healing, it is crucial to start by identifying triggers and patterns that may be holding you back. Triggers are external or internal stimuli that bring up feelings or memories associated with the trauma or difficult experiences, while patterns are repetitive behaviours or reactions that stem from past experiences. By recognizing these triggers and patterns, you can begin to understand how they influence your thoughts, emotions, and actions.

One way to identify triggers is to pay attention to your body's physical reactions when you encounter certain situations or people. Do you feel tense, anxious, or overwhelmed? These physical responses can be a sign that a trigger has been activated. Additionally, keeping a journal can help you track patterns of behaviour or thoughts that tend to repeat themselves in certain situations. By becoming more aware of these triggers and patterns, you can begin to take steps towards breaking free from their control over you.

It is important to remember that identifying triggers and patterns is not about placing blame on yourself or others. Instead, it is an opportunity to gain insight into the ways in which past trauma continues to impact your life. By approaching this process with compassion and self-reflection, you can begin to unravel the layers of hurt and pain that have been holding you back.

As you delve deeper into identifying triggers and patterns, you may notice connections between past experiences and your current struggles. This awareness can be empowering, as it allows you to take ownership of your healing journey. By recognizing the ways in which these experiences have shaped your beliefs and behaviours, you can start to challenge and reframe these ingrained patterns, paving the way for true transformation and healing.

By courageously facing your triggers and patterns, you are taking a powerful step towards reclaiming your sense of self and finding peace.

Cultivating Self-Compassion and Acceptance

In the journey towards healing self-compassion and acceptance is much needed. It is all too easy to be hard on ourselves, blaming ourselves for what happened or feeling like we are somehow at fault. But true healing begins with showing ourselves the same kindness and understanding that we would offer to a dear friend in need. To look at yourself as your own best friend, how loving and caring would you be towards them in a difficult time? That is exactly how you are to be with yourself. Show yourself some love and be patient in the process.

Self-compassion involves acknowledging our pain and suffering without judgment, and offering ourselves the comfort and support that we deserve. It means recognizing that we are human, and that we are allowed to make mistakes and have imperfections. By practicing self-compassion, we can begin to soften the harsh inner critic that often holds us back from true healing.

Acceptance is another key component in the healing process. It involves coming to terms with what has happened in the past and learning to let go of the need to control or change the past. Acceptance does not mean condoning or excusing what happened, but rather acknowledging the reality of the situation and finding a way to move forward from it.

By cultivating self-compassion and acceptance, we can begin to create a safe space within ourselves where healing can take place. We can learn to be gentle with ourselves, to forgive ourselves for past mistakes, and to embrace our own vulnerability.

So let us commit to practicing self-compassion and acceptance each day, even when it feels difficult. Let us remind ourselves that we are worthy of love and kindness, and that we deserve to heal from the pain of the past. By embracing these practices, we can take the first steps on the path towards healing and find the strength to overcome the challenges that lie ahead.

Chapter 3: Building Resilience

Developing Coping Strategies

To heal, it is essential to develop healthy coping strategies that can help you navigate through the ups and downs of the recovery process. Healthy coping strategies are like tools in your toolbox, helping you to manage difficult emotions and situations in a constructive way. By developing coping strategies, you are empowering yourself to take control of your journey and build resilience in the face of adversity.

One important coping strategy is mindfulness, which involves being present in the moment without judgment. Mindfulness can help you to stay grounded and always be connected to your emotions, allowing you to process them in a healthy way. By practicing mindfulness regularly, you can learn to observe your thoughts and feelings without getting swept away by them, leading to greater emotional stability and self-awareness.

Another effective coping strategy is self-care, which involves taking care of your physical, emotional, and mental well-being. Self-care can include activities such as exercise, journaling, spending time in nature, or engaging in hobbies that bring you joy. By prioritizing self-care, you are showing yourself love, which is an essential ingredient for healing.

It is also important to develop a support network of trusted friends, family members, or therapists who can provide you with encouragement, understanding, and guidance as you navigate through the healing process. Having a support network can help you feel less alone and more connected, providing you with a safe space to express your emotions and receive validation for your experiences.

By incorporating mindfulness, self-care, and a support network into your daily routine, you can cultivate resilience, self-awareness, and emotional well-being. By investing in yourself and your healing process, you are taking positive steps towards a brighter and more fulfilling future.

Practicing Mindfulness and Grounding Techniques

Mindfulness is the practice of being fully present in the moment, without judgment or attachment to thoughts or feelings. Through mindfulness, you can observe your thoughts and emotions with a sense of curiosity and compassion, allowing them to come and go without getting caught up in them. By cultivating mindfulness, you can develop a greater sense of self-awareness and begin to unravel the patterns of thought and behaviour that have been holding you back.

Grounding techniques are another powerful tool for trauma recovery, helping you to connect with the present moment and anchor yourself in the here and now. These techniques can include practices such as deep breathing, visualization, or physical movements that help you to feel more centred and grounded in your body. Grounding can create a sense of safety and stability within yourself, allowing you to navigate the challenges with greater ease and resilience.

Remember to approach these practices with an open heart and a spirit of curiosity. Be gentle with yourself as you explore these new ways of being, knowing that healing is a journey that unfolds at its own pace. However little progress you make it should never be underestimated. The path you are on is yours and every little step towards self-growth is a significant one.

Setting Boundaries and Prioritizing Self-Care

Setting boundaries and prioritizing self-care are essential components of the healing journey. By establishing clear boundaries, you are creating a safe space for yourself to heal and grow. It is important to recognize that you have the right to set limits on what you are comfortable with and to communicate those boundaries effectively to others. This can help you feel more empowered and in control of your experiences.

Self-care is not selfish; it is a vital part of the healing process. Taking care of yourself physically, emotionally, and mentally is crucial for your overall well-being. Prioritizing self-care means making time for activities that nourish your mind, body, and spirit. Whether it's going for a walk in nature, meditating, engaging in creative expressions such as writing, painting or doodling, spending alone time reading or finding ways to nurture yourself in your own little way is the key.

Remember that self-care is not a luxury, but a necessity. Just as you would prioritize taking care of a loved one in need, it is equally important to prioritize taking care of yourself. This means making time for rest, relaxation, and activities that bring you joy and peace. By prioritizing self-care, you are showing yourself love and compassion, which are essential ingredients for a healthy life.

Setting boundaries and prioritizing self-care also means learning to say no to things that do not serve your healing journey. This may involve saying no to toxic relationships, unhealthy habits, or situations that trigger painful memories. It is okay to put yourself first and protect your mental and emotional well-being. By setting boundaries and prioritizing self-care, you are creating a strong foundation for your healing journey and empowering yourself to make choices that align with your values and goals.

How to Set boundaries:

Identify your limits

Reflect on your physical, emotional, and mental limits. Identify situations, people, or tasks that cause stress or discomfort.

Communicate clearly

Use assertive communication to express your needs and boundaries. Be direct and respectful.

For example, "I need some time to myself after work, so I won't be available for calls."

Say NO

Practice saying no to requests or demands that exceed your limits or compromise your wellbeing. You don't need to provide elaborate explanations.

Set physical boundaries

Reflect on your personal space and privacy needs. For instance, close your office door when you need to focus, or establish certain areas at home as quiet zones.

Time boundaries

Allocate specific times for work, rest, and leisure. Stick to your schedule and avoid overcommitting to activities or responsibilities.

Emotional boundaries

Protect your emotional energy by distancing yourself from negative influences or draining relationships. Limit interactions with people who don't respect your feelings.

Digital boundaries

Limit screen time and set specific times for checking emails and social media. Turn off notifications during rest periods.

Enforce consequences

Be prepared to follow through with consequences if your boundaries are crossed. For example, if someone repeatedly disrespects your time, reconsider your involvement with them.

Prioritizing self-care:

Physical exercise

Incorporate exercise into your routine. Activities like walking, yoga, or swimming can improve physical health and reduce stress. Physical exercise has been proven to boost dopamine and serotonin levels which can improve mood.

Healthy eating

Maintain a balanced diet rich in fruits, vegetables, whole grains, and lean proteins. Stay hydrated and limit intake of processed foods and sugars.

Adequate Sleep

Aim for 7-9 hours of sleep per night. Create a relaxing bedtime routine and sleep-friendly environment.

Mindfulness and relaxation

Practice mindfulness techniques such as meditation, deep breathing, or progressive muscle relaxation to reduce stress and increase relaxation.

Hobbies and interests

Dedicate time to activities you enjoy and that bring you joy, whether it's reading, painting, gardening, or playing a musical instrument.

Social connections

Nurture relationships with supportive friends and family. Spend time with people who uplift and energize you

Mental health

Seek therapy or counselling if needed. Regularly engage in practices that support mental wellbeing, such as journaling or self-reflection.

Time management

Plan and prioritize tasks effectively. Use tools like planners or apps to organize your schedule and avoid overloading yourself.

Set Realistic goals

Break down larger tasks into smaller, manageable steps. Celebrate your achievements, no matter how small.

Self compassion

Treat yourself with kindness and understanding. Avoid self-criticism and acknowledge your efforts and progress.

Resource Books: "Set Boundaries, Find Peace" by Nedra Glover Tawwab, "The Art of Extreme Self-Care" by Cheryl Richardson. "You can Heal your Life" by Louise Hay, "The Alchemist" by Paulo Coelho.

Apps: Headspace, Calm, Insight Timer for mindfulness, Trello for time management.

Therapists and coaches: Seek guidance from professionals who specialize in boundary-setting and self-care strategies.

Chapter 4: Processing and Expressing Emotions

Journaling and Creative Expression

Journaling and creative expression can be powerful tools for healing from trauma. These techniques help individuals process emotions, gain insights, and find meaning in their experiences. Here are some specific methods and prompts tailored to trauma healing.

Journaling techniques for Trauma healing:

Free writing

Write continuously for a set period (10-20 minutes) without worrying about grammar or structure. Let your thoughts ow freely. Prompt: "Describe your feelings today. What memories or images come up?"

Dialogue journaling

Write a conversation between yourself and a supportive figure (real or imagined). This can help externalize and process difficult emotions.

Prompt: "Have a dialogue with your inner child about the trauma. What does your inner child need to hear?"

Emotion-Focused journaling

Focus on exploring and naming your emotions related to the trauma.

Prompt: "What emotions are you feeling right now? How do they relate to your trauma?"

Gratitude Journal

Write about things you are grateful for, which can help shift your focus to positive aspects of your life.

Prompt: "What are three things you are grateful for today, despite the trauma?"

Self-Compassion journaling

Write kind and supportive messages to yourself.

Prompt: "Write a letter to yourself offering compassion and understanding for what you've been through."

Reflective journaling

Reflect on how the trauma has impacted you and how you have grown or what you have learned from the experience.

Prompt: "How has the trauma shaped who you are today? What

strengths have you discovered in yourself?"

Creative Expression through journaling:

Art

Combine writing with drawing, painting, or collage to express feelings and memories related to the trauma.

Prompt: "Create an image that represents your healing journey."

Collage

Use images and words from magazines or printouts to create a collage that expresses your emotions and experiences.

Prompt: "Make a collage that depicts your inner world."

Poetry and Creative writing

Write poems, short stories, or letters that reflect your trauma and healing process. Prompt: "Write a poem about your journey from darkness to light.

Music and Sound

Create a playlist of songs that resonate with your emotions or compose your own music.

Prompt: "Choose a song that reflects your mood and write about why it speaks to you."

Photography

Take photos that capture your emotions or significant moments for positive imprinting.

Prompt: "Create a photo series that tells the story of your recovery."

Dance and Movement

Use movement or dance to express and release emotions stored in your body.

Prompt: "Create a dance that represents the different stages of your healing journey"

Sculpting and Crafting

Use materials like clay, wood, or fabric to create sculptures or crafts that symbolize your experiences and emotions.

Prompt: "Sculpt an object that represents you and another that symbolizes hope and healing for you."

Tips for Effective Practice:

Consistency

Set aside regular time for journaling and creative expression. This could be daily or several times a week.

Safety and Comfort

Create a safe and comfortable environment for your practice. Ensure privacy and minimize distractions.

Non-Judgement

Approach your journaling and creative work without self-criticism. Focus on the process, not the result.

Mindfulness

Begin your sessions with mindfulness exercises, such as deep breathing or grounding techniques, to centre yourself.

Professional support

Consider working with a therapist who specializes in trauma to guide you through these practices if you can.

Seeking Support from Therapists or Support Groups

In times of deep emotional pain and trauma, seeking support from therapists or support groups can be a crucial step on the path to healing. These professionals are trained to provide guidance, understanding, and tools to help you navigate your journey towards healing. By reaching out for help, you are taking a crucial step towards reclaiming your mental and emotional well-being.

Therapists are skilled in helping individuals process their past traumas in a safe and supportive environment. They can provide you with coping strategies, tools for managing triggers, and techniques for processing dif cult emotions. Through therapy, you can gain a deeper understanding of yourself and your experiences, allowing you to heal and grow in ways you never thought possible.

Support groups offer a unique opportunity to connect with others who have experienced similar traumas. Sharing your story with others who understand can be incredibly validating and empowering. Together, you can learn from each other's experiences and provide each other with a sense of community and belonging.

It's important to remember that seeking support from therapists or support groups is not a sign of weakness, but rather a courageous and empowering step. It takes strength and courage to confront your past traumas and work towards healing them.

Understanding the Importance of Emotional Release

Understanding the importance of emotional release is a crucial step on the path to healing. Emotions play a significant role in how we experience and process our trauma, and allowing ourselves to release these pent-up feelings is essential for our overall well-being.

Emotional release is a powerful tool because it allows us to acknowledge and express the pain and hurt that we have been holding onto. When we suppress our emotions, they can manifest in physical and psychological symptoms, leading to further distress and discomfort. By releasing these emotions, we can create space for healing and transformation to occur within ourselves.

Through emotional release, we can also gain a deeper understanding of ourselves and our trauma. By allowing ourselves to feel and express our emotions, we can uncover the root causes of our pain and begin to address them in a healthy and productive way.

Chapter 5: Healing Through Forgiveness

Forgiving Yourself and Others

Forgiving yourself and others is a crucial step on the path to healing from past trauma. It may seem like a daunting task, but it is essential for moving forward and finding peace within yourself.

Forgiveness is not about condoning the actions of others or forgetting the pain they caused you. It is about releasing the hold that anger and resentment have on your heart and mind, allowing yourself to heal and move on from the past.

When we hold onto grudges and harbour resentment towards others, we are only hurting ourselves. The negative emotions we keep bottled up inside can manifest as physical ailments, mental health issues, and a general sense of unease. By choosing to forgive those who have wronged us, we are freeing ourselves from the chains of the past and opening space for healing and growth.

Forgiveness is a gift we give ourselves. It is a way of showing compassion and kindness to our own hearts, allowing ourselves to let go of the pain and suffering that has held us back for so long. By forgiving others, we are also releasing ourselves from the burden of carrying around anger and bitterness. It is a liberating experience that can bring about a sense of peace and freedom that is truly transformative.

Forgiving yourself is just as important as forgiving others. It is easy to hold onto guilt and shame for past mistakes, but doing so only serves to keep us stuck in a cycle of self-doubt and self-blame. By practicing self-forgiveness, we are acknowledging our humanity and allowing ourselves the grace to learn and grow from our past actions. It is a powerful act of self-love and acceptance.

Forgiveness is a key component. It is a way of honouring our own inner strength and resilience, and choosing to let go of the pain and suffering that has held us back for so long. By forgiving yourself and others, you are opening yourself up to the possibility of true healing and transformation. Embrace forgiveness as a powerful tool on your path to healing.

Steps to Facilitate forgiveness:

Acknowledge and Recognise the Pain

Acknowledge the hurt and pain caused by the person or event. Understand the impact it has had on your life.

Identify your Emotions

Identify the specific emotions you feel as a result of the hurt, such as anger, sadness, or betrayal.

Understand Forgiveness to Clarify Misconceptions

Understand that forgiveness does not mean condoning the behaviour, excusing the action, or forgetting the incident.

Realise the Benefits

Focus on the benefits of forgiveness for your own well-being, rather than for the person who hurt you.

Decide to Forgive/Make a Conscious Choice

Forgiveness is a deliberate decision. Decide that you want to forgive for your own peace and healing.

Commit to the Process

Understand that forgiveness is a process that may take time and effort.

Empathize with the Offender/Consider their Perspective

Try to understand the situation from the offender's point of view. This doesn't justify their actions but can provide insight.

Recognize Human Imperfection

Acknowledge that everyone makes mistakes, and that people can change.

Release Negative Emotions to Express your Feelings

Use journaling, talking to a trusted friend, or therapy to express and release your feelings.

Practice Letting Go

Engage in mindfulness or meditation to help release the grip of negative emotions.

Seek Resolution/Communicate if Possible

If it feels safe and appropriate, communicate with the person who hurt you to express your feelings and seek closure.

Accept what you Cannot Change

Sometimes, direct communication isn't possible or safe. In such cases, focus on accepting the situation as it is.

Forgive yourself /Self-Forgiveness

Often, forgiving yourself for perceived mistakes or weaknesses is a crucial part of the healing process.

Practice Compassion and Kindness

Practice compassion towards yourself and others. This can help soften feelings of anger and resentment.

Perform Acts of Kindness

Engage in acts of kindness and service to shift your focus from pain to positive action. Acts of service are acts of unconditional love and it can help in feeling love for yourself and others

Cultivating Empathy and Understanding

Empathy allows us to connect with others on a deeper level, to truly understand their experiences and emotions.

By understanding our own emotions, thoughts, and behaviours, we can begin to unravel the complex web of trauma that has impacted our lives. It allows us to make sense of our experiences and find meaning in our pain. It is through understanding that we can begin to release the grip that trauma has on our lives and move towards a place of healing and wholeness.

Practicing empathy and understanding also allows us to build stronger connections with others who have experienced trauma. By listening with an open heart and mind, we can offer support and validation to those who are struggling.

As we cultivate empathy and understanding in ourselves and for others, we begin to be grateful for the experiences that have shaped us. We can transform our pain into purpose and our wounds into wisdom.

You will not only heal yourself by practicing understanding and empathy but also create a ripple effect of healing and transformation in the world around you.

Chapter 6: Moving Forward and Thriving

Setting Goals and Intentions for Healing

When we take the time to set clear intentions and goals for our healing journey, we are actively participating in our own healing process. By setting goals, we are creating a roadmap for ourselves, guiding us towards a life of peace, healing, and self-discovery.

One of the first steps in setting goals for healing is to reflect on where we are currently in our healing journey. Take the time to acknowledge the progress you have already made and the areas in which you still need to grow. By taking stock of where you are, you can begin to set realistic and achievable goals for your healing process.

Setting intentions is equally important in the healing journey. Intentions are the guiding principles that shape our actions and decisions. By setting intentions for healing, we are declaring to ourselves and the universe our commitment to our own well-being. Intentions can be as simple as "I intend to practice self-care daily" or "I intend to be kind to myself throughout this healing process."

When setting goals and intentions for healing, it is important to be specific and concrete. Vague goals such as "I want to feel better" are less effective than specific goals such as "I want to attend therapy once a week" or "I want to practice mindfulness for 10 minutes each day." By being specific, we can measure our progress and celebrate our successes along the way. Trust in the process, be gentle with yourself, and know that you are capable of healing from past trauma through self-work.

Embracing Growth and Transformation

In this subchapter, we explore the powerful journey of embracing growth and transformation on the path to healing from past trauma through self-work. It is important to recognize that healing is not a linear process, but rather a series of ups and downs, twists and turns, that ultimately lead us to a place of greater self-awareness and resilience. It is through this process that we can truly begin to transform our pain into power and our wounds into wisdom.

As we embark on this journey of self-work, it is crucial to approach it with an open mind and a willingness to embrace change. Growth and transformation require us to step outside of our comfort zones, to confront our fears and insecurities head-on, and to challenge the limiting beliefs that hold us back from reaching our full potential. It is only through this process of self-exploration and introspection that we can begin to release the grip of trauma on our lives and move towards a place of healing and wholeness.

One of the key aspects of embracing growth and transformation is the practice of self-compassion. It is important to treat ourselves with kindness and understanding as we navigate the challenges of healing from past trauma. By cultivating a sense of self-love and acceptance, we can begin to heal the wounds of the past and create a new narrative for our lives. It is through this practice of self-compassion that we can begin to let go of shame, guilt, and self-blame, and move towards a place of forgiveness and self-empowerment.

Another important aspect of embracing growth and transformation is the willingness to seek support and guidance from others. Healing from past trauma can be a daunting and overwhelming process, and it is important to recognize that we do not have to go through it alone. Seeking out the help of therapists, support groups, and other resources can provide us with the tools and strategies we need to navigate the challenges of healing and transformation. By surrounding ourselves with a strong support network, we can find the courage and strength to continue on our path to healing.

In conclusion, embracing growth and transformation on the path to healing from past trauma through self-work is a profound and transformative journey. It requires courage, vulnerability, and a willingness to confront our deepest wounds and fears. But it is through this process that we can begin to release the grip of trauma on our lives, and move towards a place of healing, wholeness, and self-empowerment. By approaching this journey with an open heart and a commitment to self-compassion. Let us embrace the journey ahead with hope, courage, and a steadfast belief in our ability to heal and transform.

Celebrating Your Progress and Success

Remember, healing is not a linear process, and there will be ups and downs along the way. But by celebrating your progress, you are reminding yourself of the strength and resilience you possess.

When you take the time to celebrate your progress, you are also reinforcing positive behaviours and actions that have led to your growth and healing. By acknowledging your successes, no matter how small they may seem, you are motivating yourself to continue the path to healing. It's a way of saying to yourself, "I see you; I appreciate you, and I am proud of you."

One way to celebrate your progress and success is to create a ritual or ceremony that honours your achievements. This could be as simple as lighting a candle and taking a moment of silence to reflect on how far you've come. Or you could write yourself a letter of congratulations, outlining all the milestones you've reached on your healing journey. By creating a ritual around celebrating your progress, you are giving yourself the space and time to truly appreciate the work you've done.

Another way to celebrate your progress is to share your successes with others. Remember, healing is not a solo journey, and by sharing your progress with others, you are inviting in a sense of connection and camaraderie. It could also inspire others to do the same by seeing your courage and strength.

Chapter 7: Sustaining Your Healing Journey

Practicing Daily Rituals and Habits:

Read and Research

Read books, articles and research on healing and personal growth to stay informed and inspired.

Mindfulness Meditation

Regularly practice mindfulness meditation to stay present and reduce anxiety.

Grounding Techniques

Use grounding techniques, such as focusing on the physical sensations of your surroundings, to stay connected to the present moment.

Self-Reflection

Regularly take time to reflect on your growth, weaknesses and challenges.

Set Aside Time for Prayer

Dedicate a specific time each day for prayer, creating a routine that provides consistency and structure. Focus on prayers of gratitude, acknowledging and appreciating the positive aspects in your life and the progress in your healing journey.

Acknowledge Achievements

Recognise and celebrate your achievements, no matter how small.

Acknowledging Your Strength and Courage:

It takes immense bravery to confront the pain and wounds of the past, and by recognizing your own resilience, you empower yourself to continue on the path to recovery. You have already taken the first step towards healing by acknowledging the need for self-work, and now it is time to honour the inner strength that has carried you through the darkest moments.

Write down your accomplishments, no matter how small they may seem, and reflect on the progress you have made in your healing journey. By recognizing and honouring your own resilience, you cultivate a sense of self-worth and empowerment that will carry you through the darkest moments. Remember, you are stronger than you think, and you have the power within you to heal and thrive.

In the words of Maya Angelou, "I can be changed by what happens to me. But I refuse to be reduced by it." Embrace your strength, honour your courage, and continue on the path to healing with a sense of purpose and determination. You can transform your pain into power.

Committing to Continued Self-Work

and Growth:

Short-Term goals

Break down larger objectives into smaller, manageable steps to stay motivated and track your progress.

Long-Term goals

Keep sight of your overall healing goals to maintain direction and purpose.

Friends and Family

Surround yourself with supportive friends and family members.

Identify your Purpose

Understand your purpose and what motivates you to heal. This can provide direction and strength.

Align with your purpose

Engage in activities that align with your values and purpose to maintain a sense of fulfilment.

Adapt to Change

Be open to adjusting your strategies and goals as needed. Healing is a dynamic purpose that may require flexibility.

Accept Setbacks

Understand that setbacks are a neutral part of the healing journey. Learn from them and keep moving forward.

Embracing the Possibility of a Brighter Future:

Positive Self-Talk

Practise positive self-talk to counteract negative thoughts. Affirmations can help reinforce a positive mindset.

Identify your "Why"

Clearly understand why your goals are important to you. Connecting your actions to a larger purpose can provide motivation.

Positive Influence

Surround yourself with people and things that inspire and motivate you.

Productivity Apps

Use apps and tools to track your goals and progress. Apps like Todoist, Trello, Finch and Habit tracker can help you stay organised and motivated.

Limit Distractions

Use technology to limit distractions such as setting screen time limits or using focus apps.

Watch Motivational content online

Watch motivational videos by life coaches, Watch TED talks, or listen to podcasts that inspire you.

Avoid Perfectionism

Recognise that perfectionism is not

www.ingramcontent.com/pod-product-compliance
Lightning Source LLC
Chambersburg PA
CBHW061327140726
47998CB00007B/2589